GUITAR/FLUTE DUETS ON CELTIC FAVORITES

MB21831
BY VOLKER LUFT

Free flute solo part download available online!
Visit: www.melbay.com/21831

BILL'S MUSIC SHELF

Schell Music

Visit us on the Web at www.melbay.com or www.billsmusicshelf.com

Playing tips

"Celtic Twins" is a collection of traditional English, Scottish and Irish fiddle tunes. They are divided into four categories according to their different characters:

Waltzes, Hornpipes, Reels and Jigs.

Each of these dances has its own stylistic peculiarities which need to be taken into consideration.

1. Waltzes are played at a moderate, stately tempo. The first beat of each bar (in 3/4 time) is always slightly accentuated.

2. Jigs: We differentiate between slow jigs (dotted quarter note = moderate tempo/andante), double jigs (dotted quarter note = medium tempo/moderato) and slip jigs (dotted quarter note = lively tempo/allegro). Jigs are usually written in 6/8 time, the 1st and 4th eighth notes are accented.

3. Reels are usually played at a very fast tempo (prestissimo), though one now and again hears reels in a moderate tempo. Written eighth notes are played bouncy, which means that as in jazz they are given a triplet or ternary swing feel by playing the first of each pair twice as long as the second. This also applies to hornpipes.

4. Hornpipes are fast pieces in 4/4 time (presto). The notes which fall on the quarter beats are slightly accented and the eighth notes are played bouncy and swinging, as in the case of reels.

This edition is scored for the combination of guitar and flute, plus an extra part for flute. The flute parts can also be played on the recorder. In passages which lie outside the easily playable range on the recorder, an alternative part for this instrument is included.

The embellishments as notated here (trills, anticipated notes) simply offer one of the many possible options in each case. I recommend that you practice the pieces "clean" first of all and add the embellishments later, when you're sure of the tune.

Content

Notes on the Execution of Embellishments:

Turn

Trill

Single trill or inverted mordent

or single trill with accidental

Mordent (single trill with lower secondary note)

Fast anticipated notes

CELTIC TWINS
guitar part/ score

The Cinderella Waltz

Waltz

arranged by Volker Luft

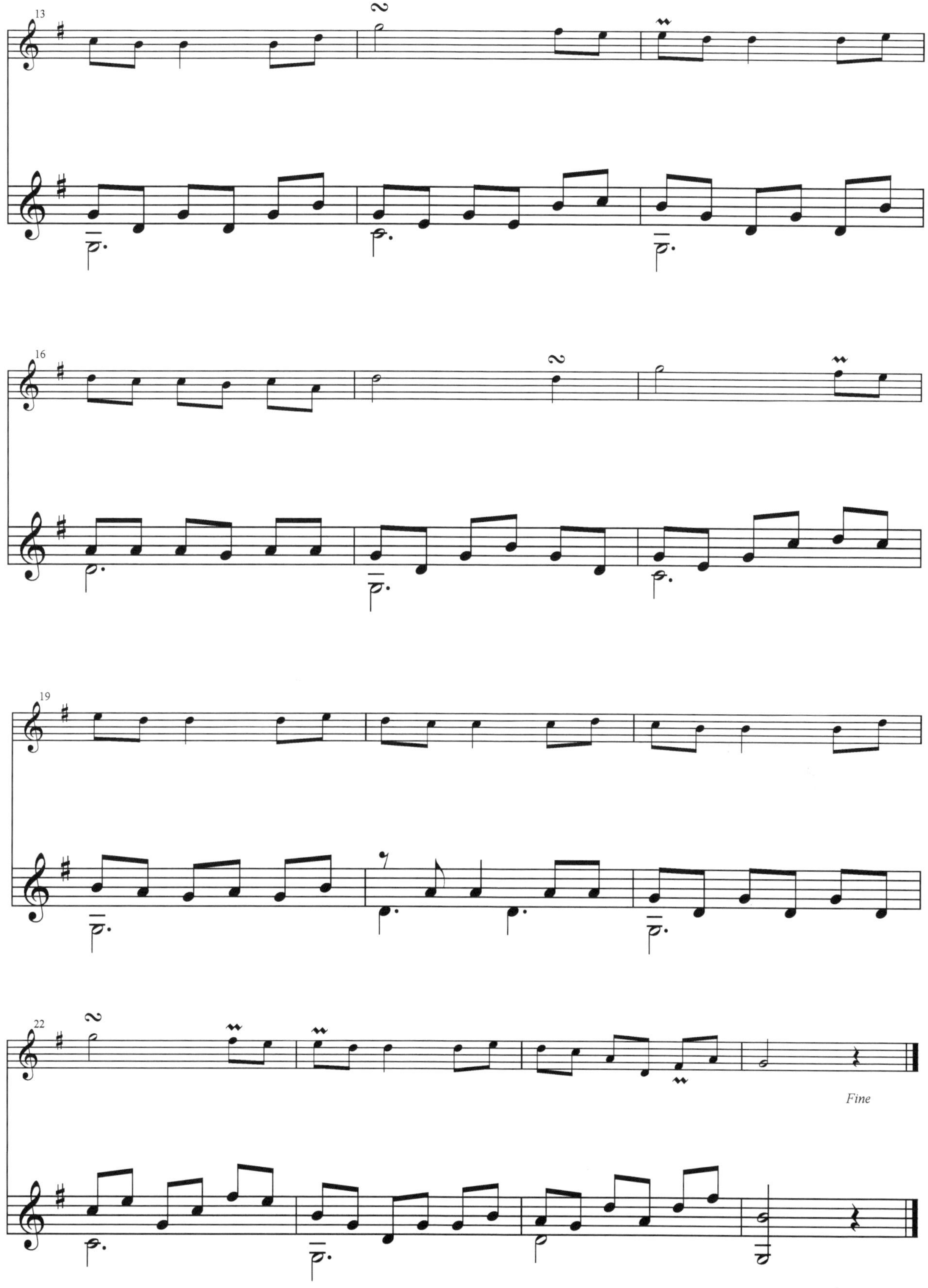
13
16
19
22
Fine

My Lodging's On The Cold Grown

Waltz

arranged by Volker Luft

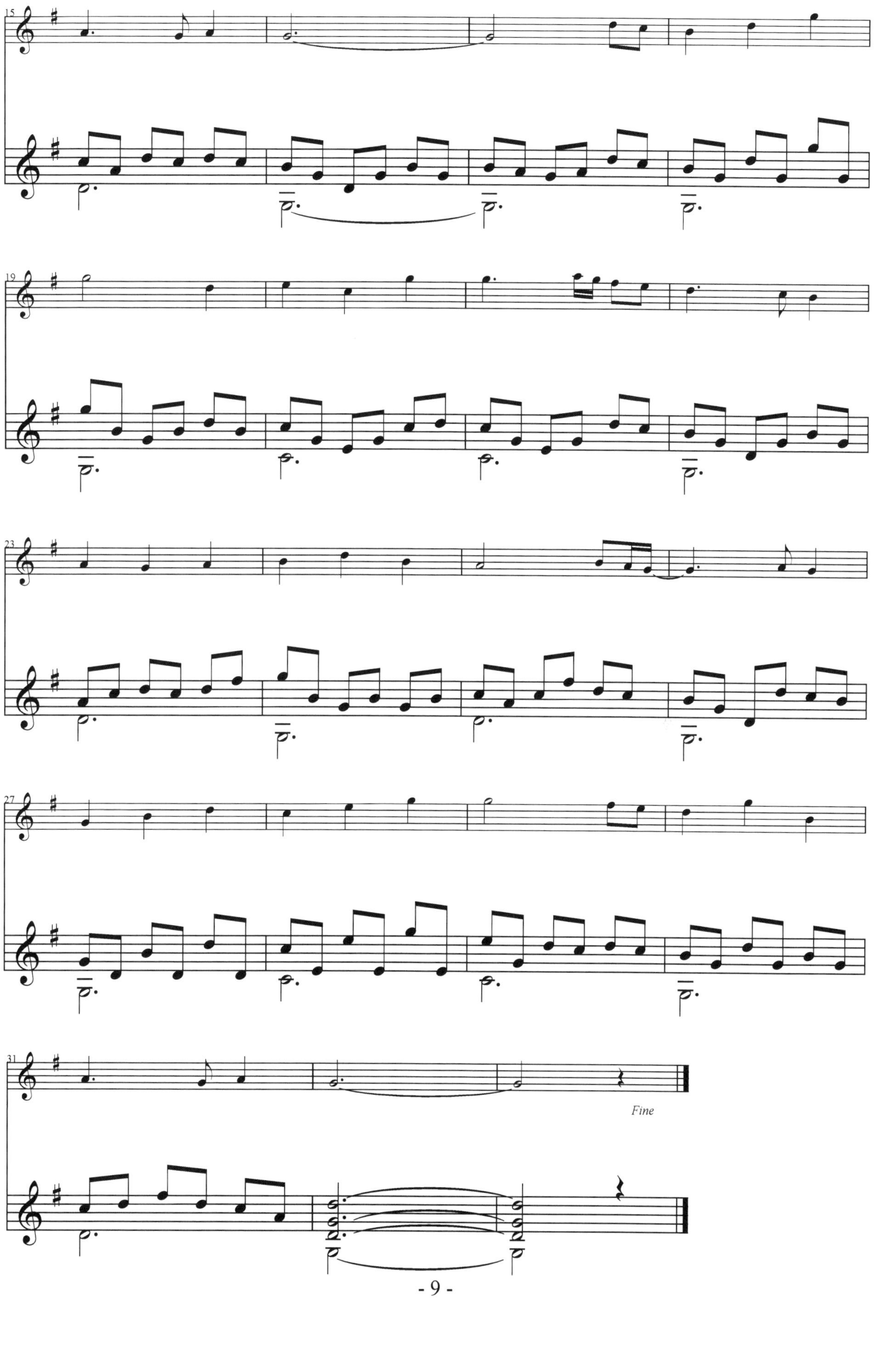
15
19
23
27
31
Fine

Tripping Upstairs

Jig

arranged by Volker Luft

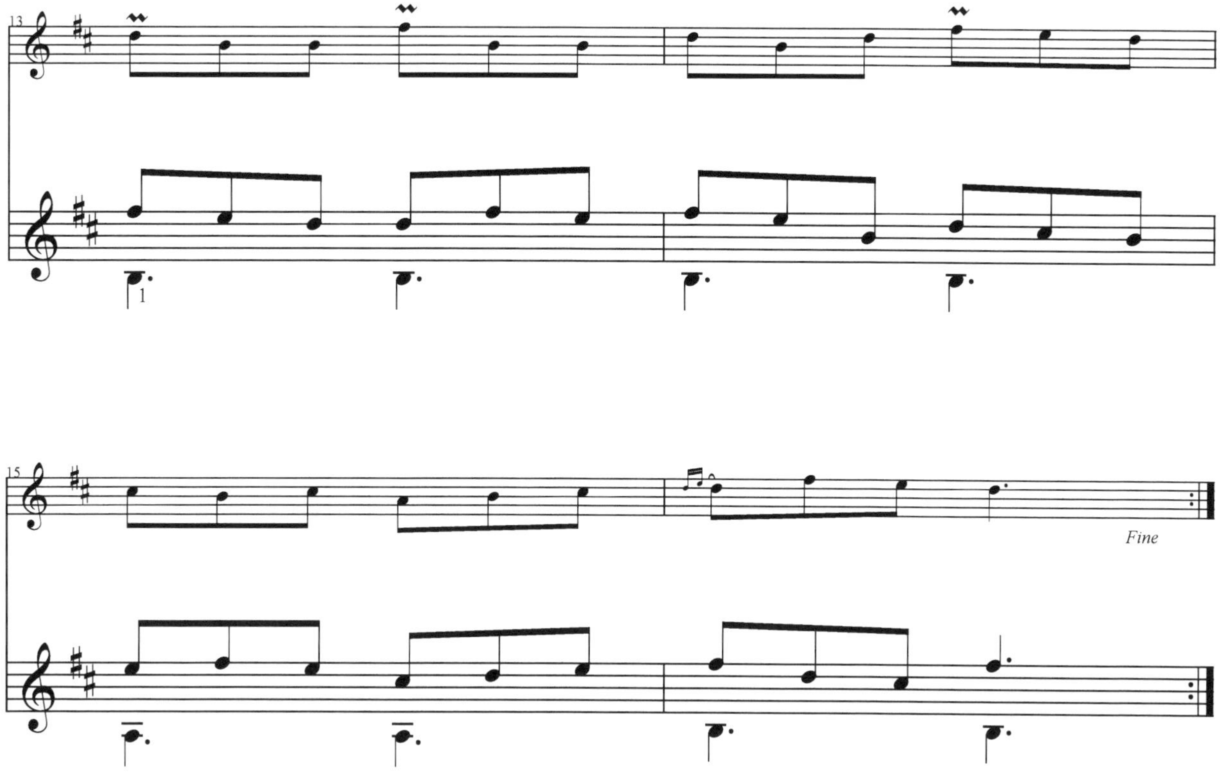
13
1
15
Fine

Muckin O' Geordie's Byre

Jig

arranged by Volker Luft

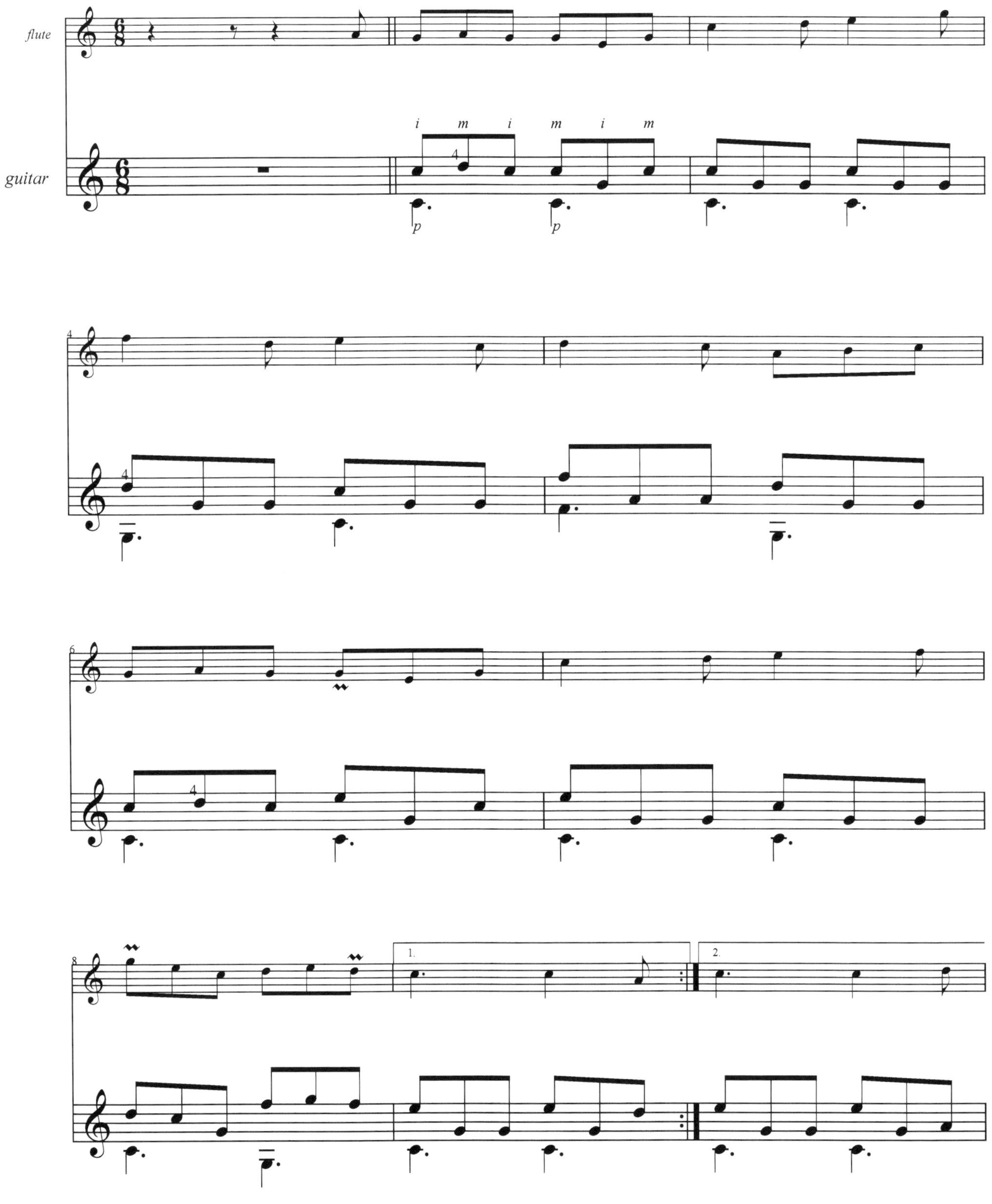

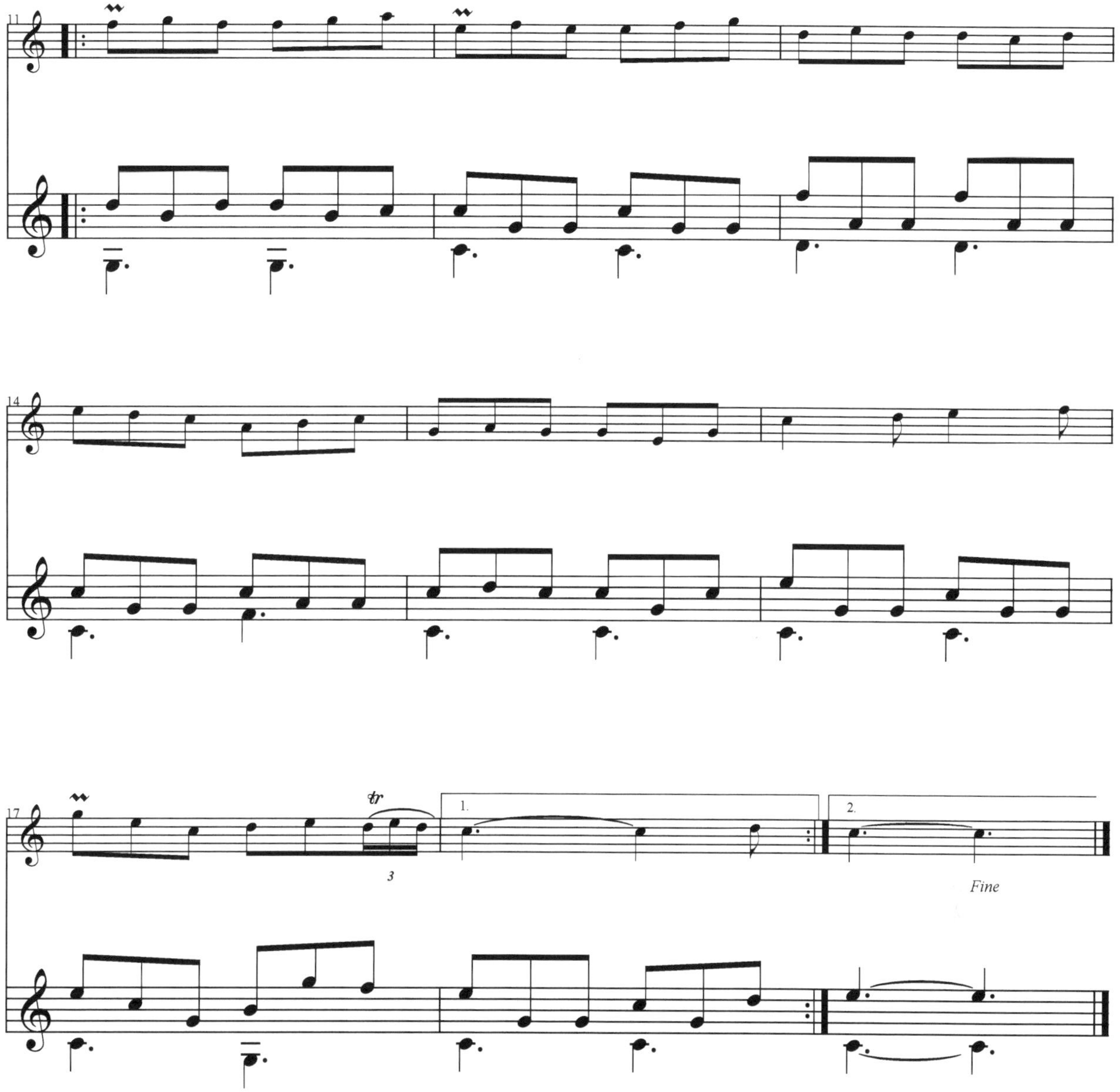
1.
2.
Fine

Lanigan's Ball

Jig

arranged by Volker Luft

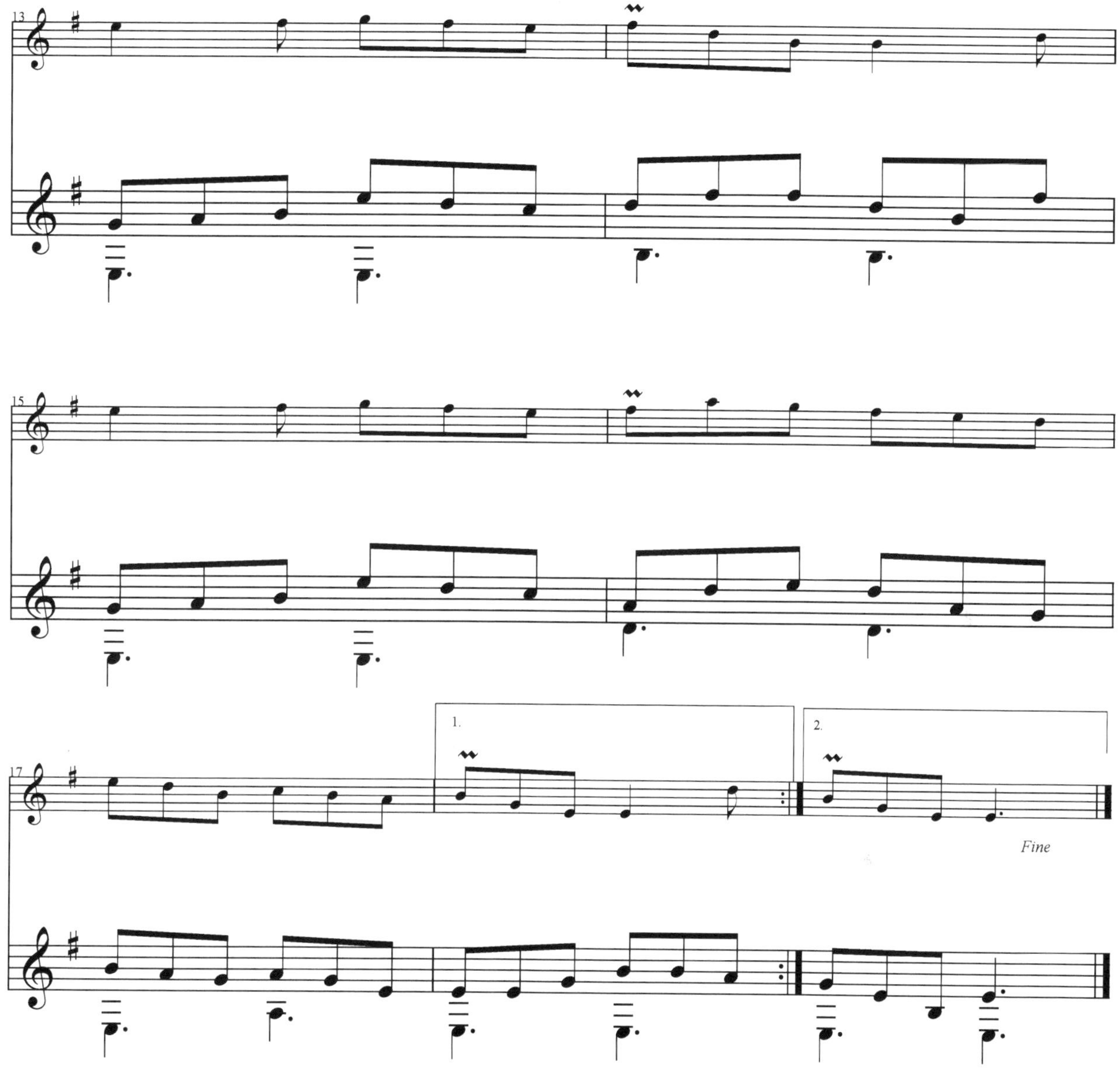
13
15
17
1.
2.
Fine

The Scotchman's Bonnet

Reel

arranged by Volker Luft

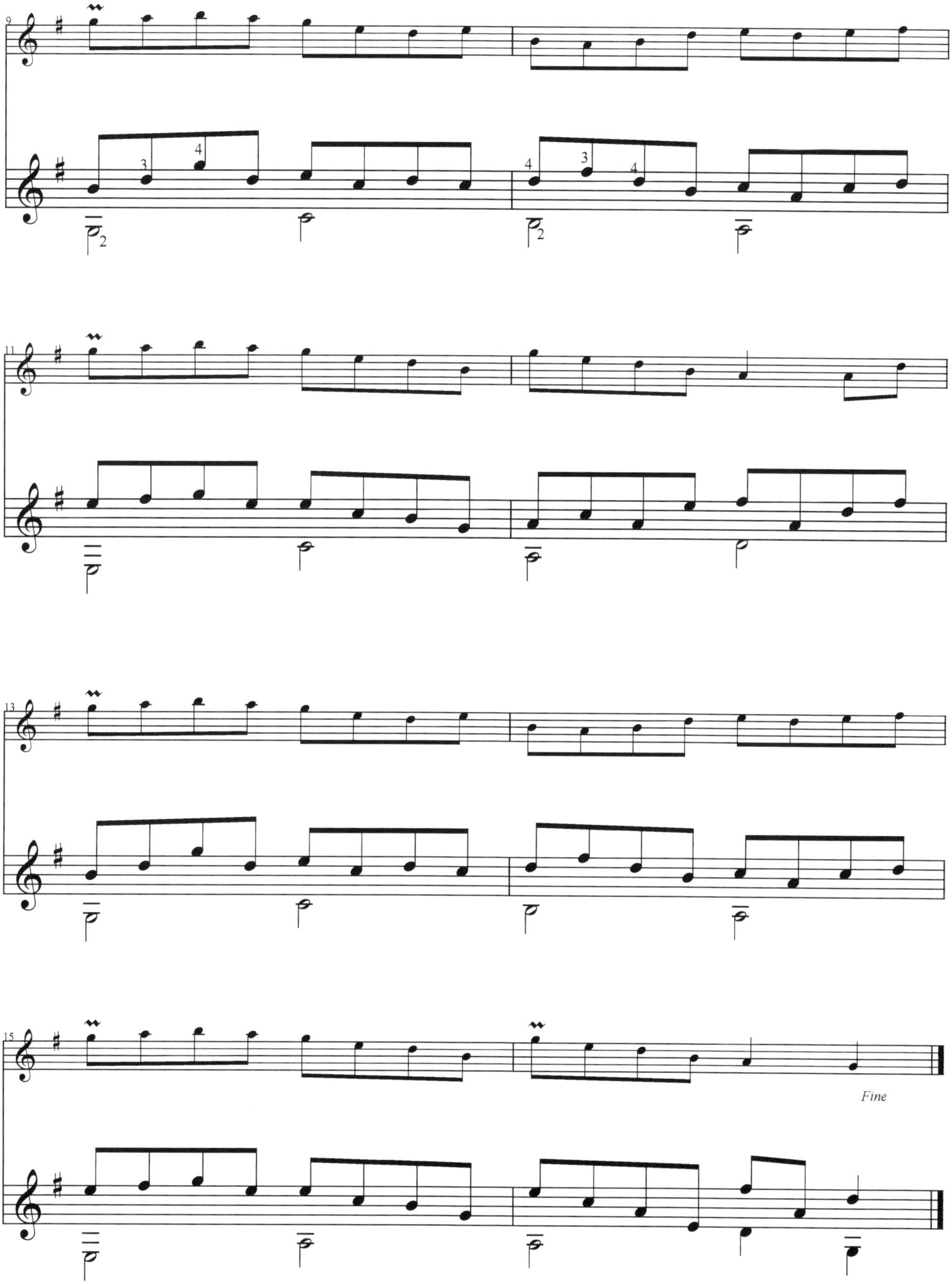
Fine

Captain Mcintosh

Reel

arranged by Volker Luft

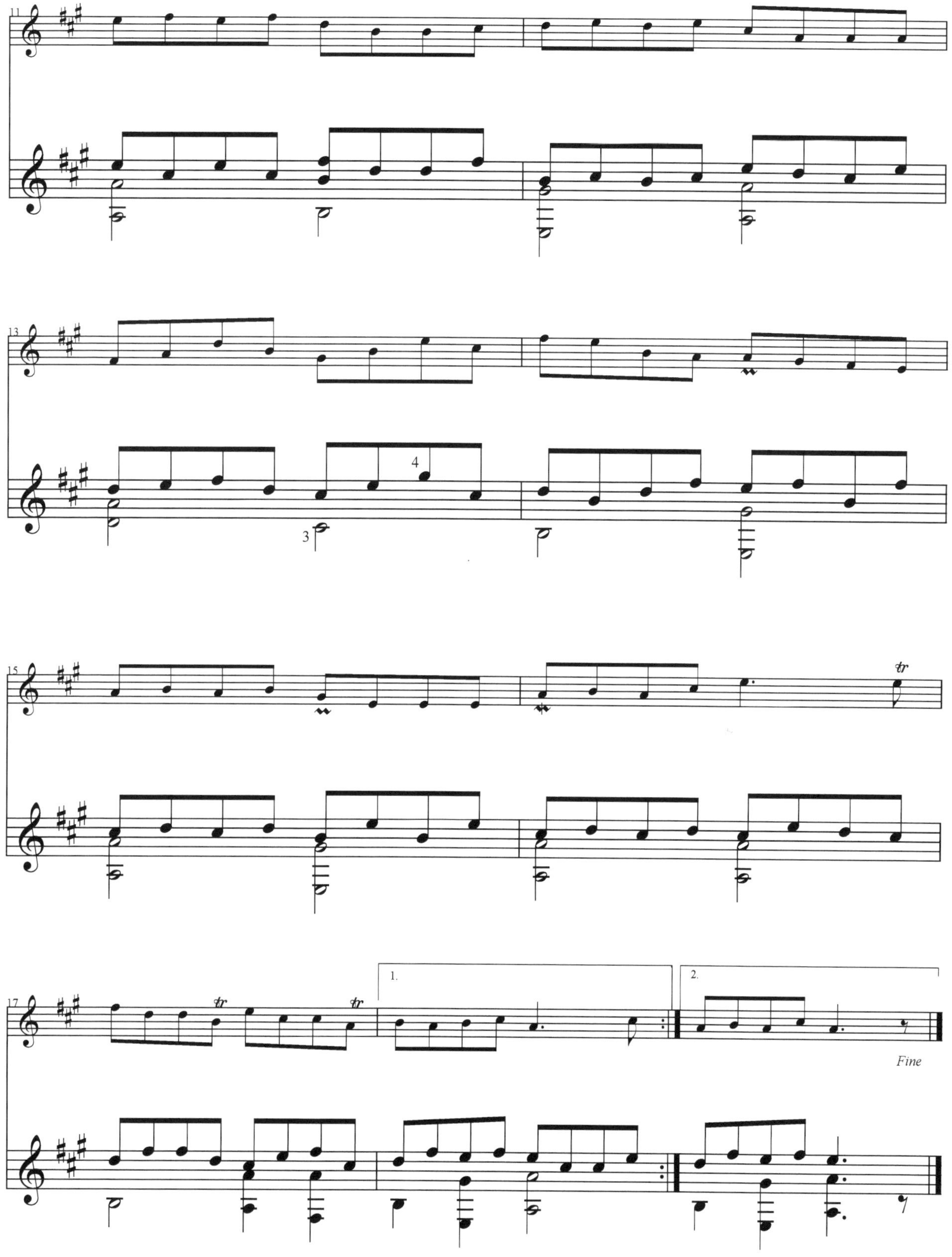

1.
2.
Fine

The Bonnie Lad

Reel

arranged by Volker Luft

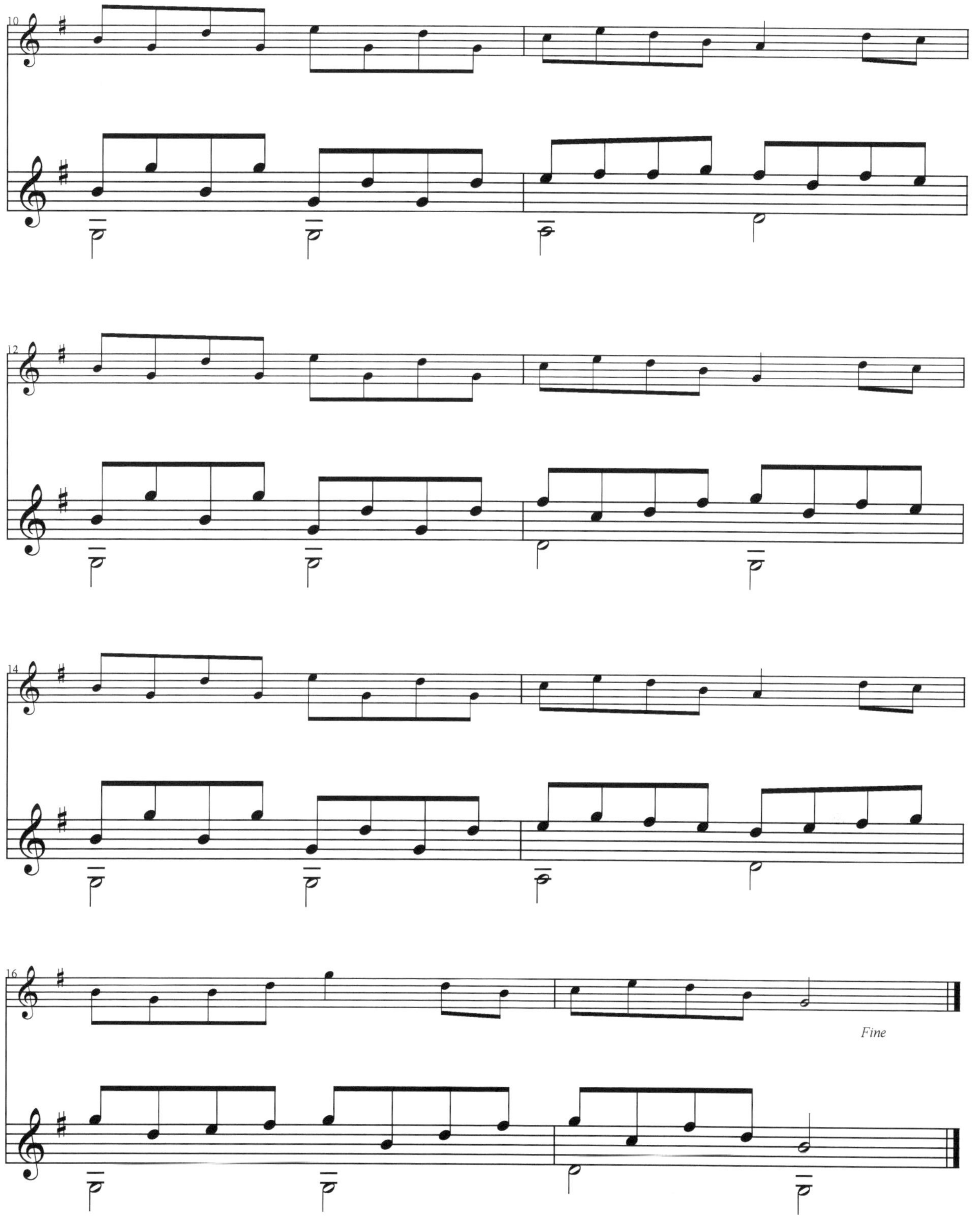
10
12
14
16
Fine

The Fairy Reel

arranged by Volker Luft

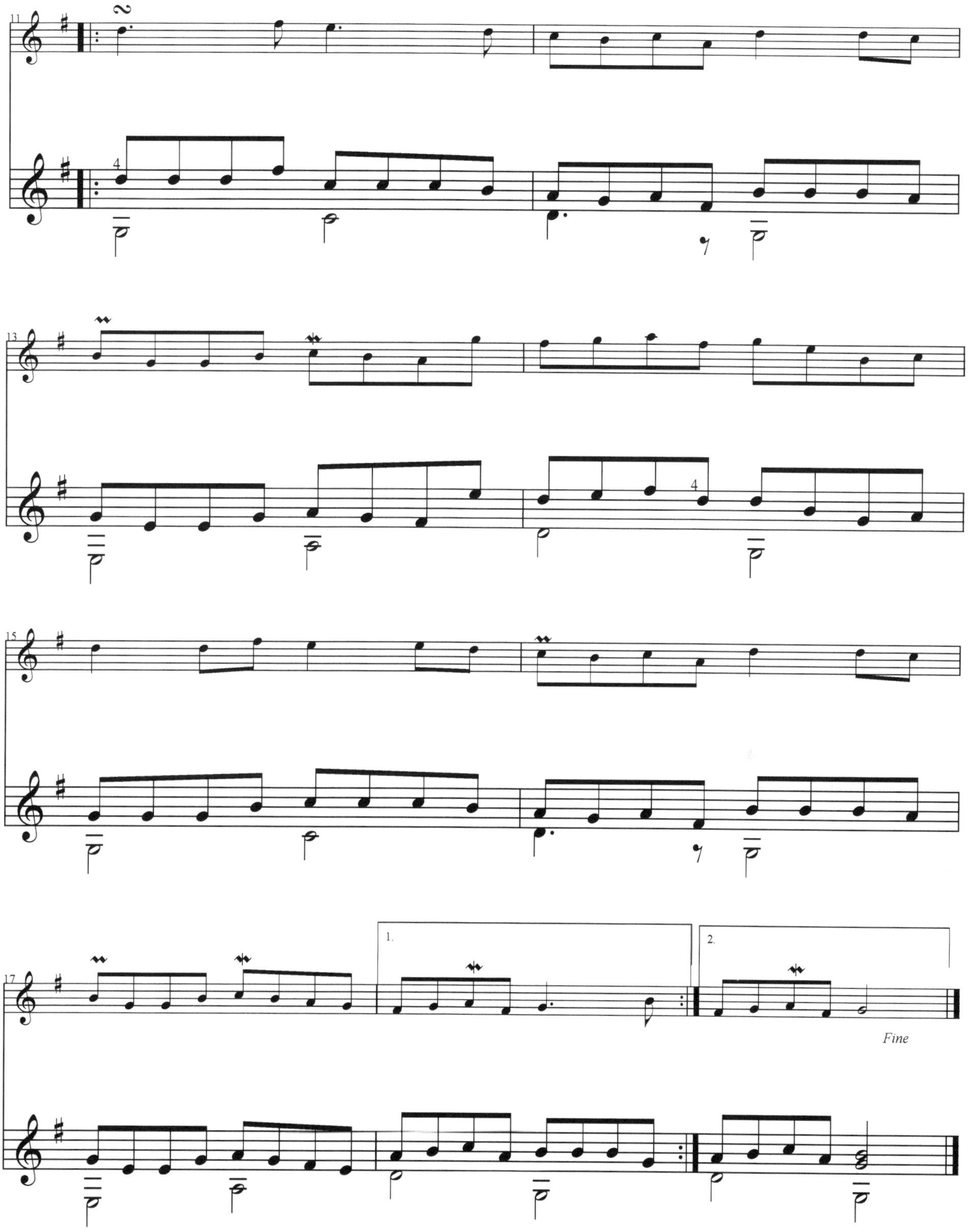
11
13
15
17
1.
2.
Fine

Lochaber Reel

arranged by Volker Luft

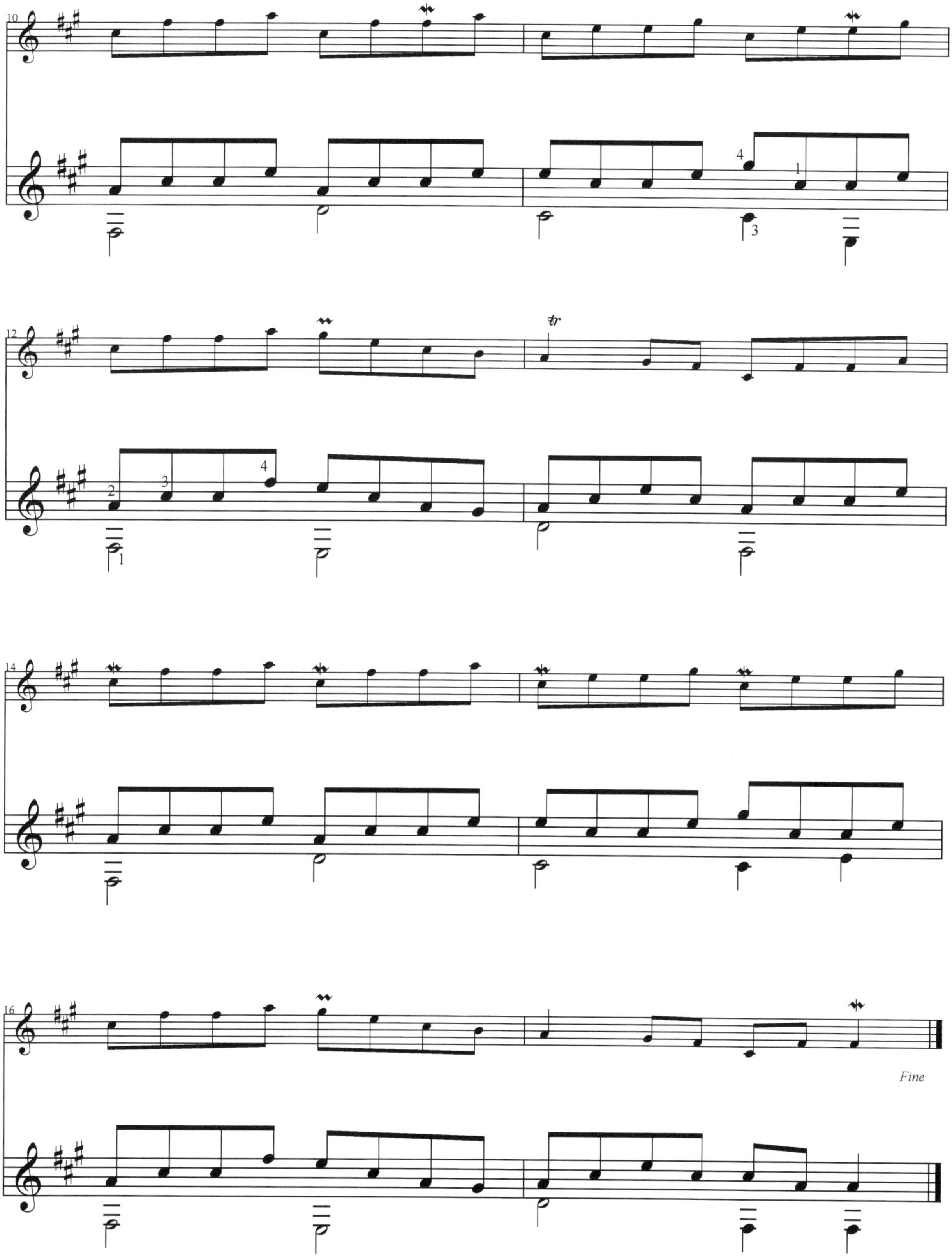
tr
Fine

My Own Whym

Reel

arranged by Volker Luft

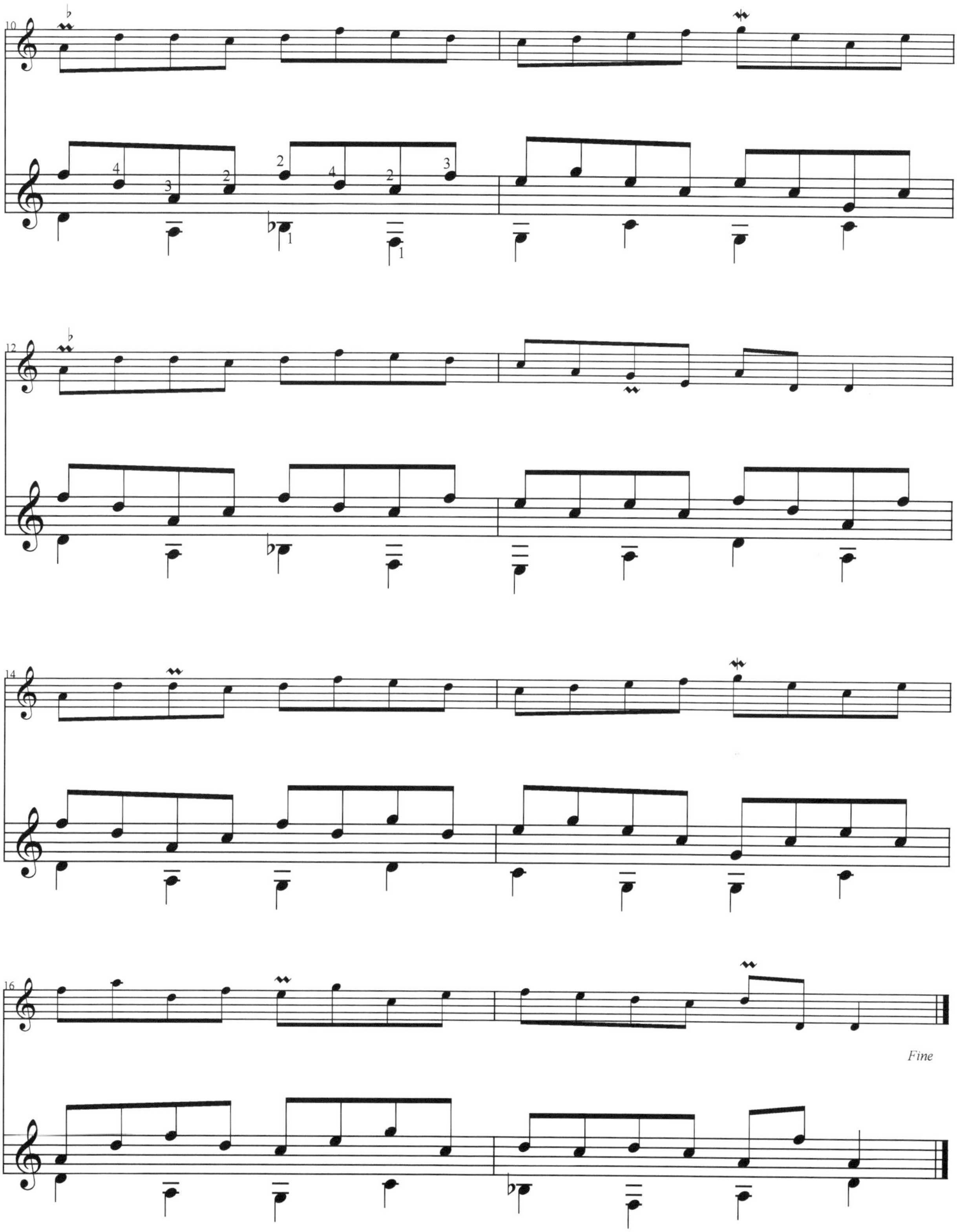
10
12
14
16
Fine

Lady Corbett's Reel

arranged by Volker Luft

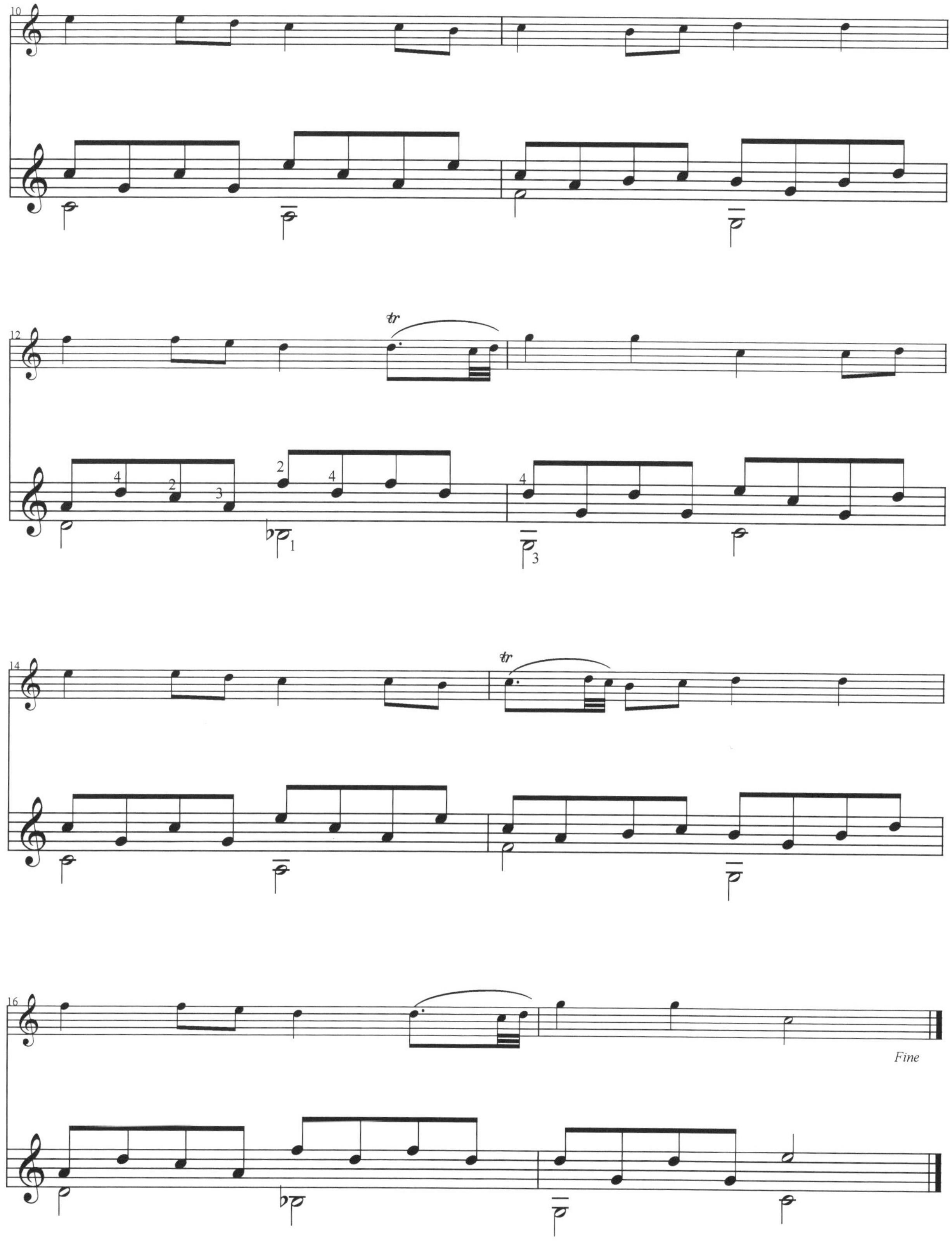
Fine

The High Road Linton

Hornpipe

arranged by Volker Luft

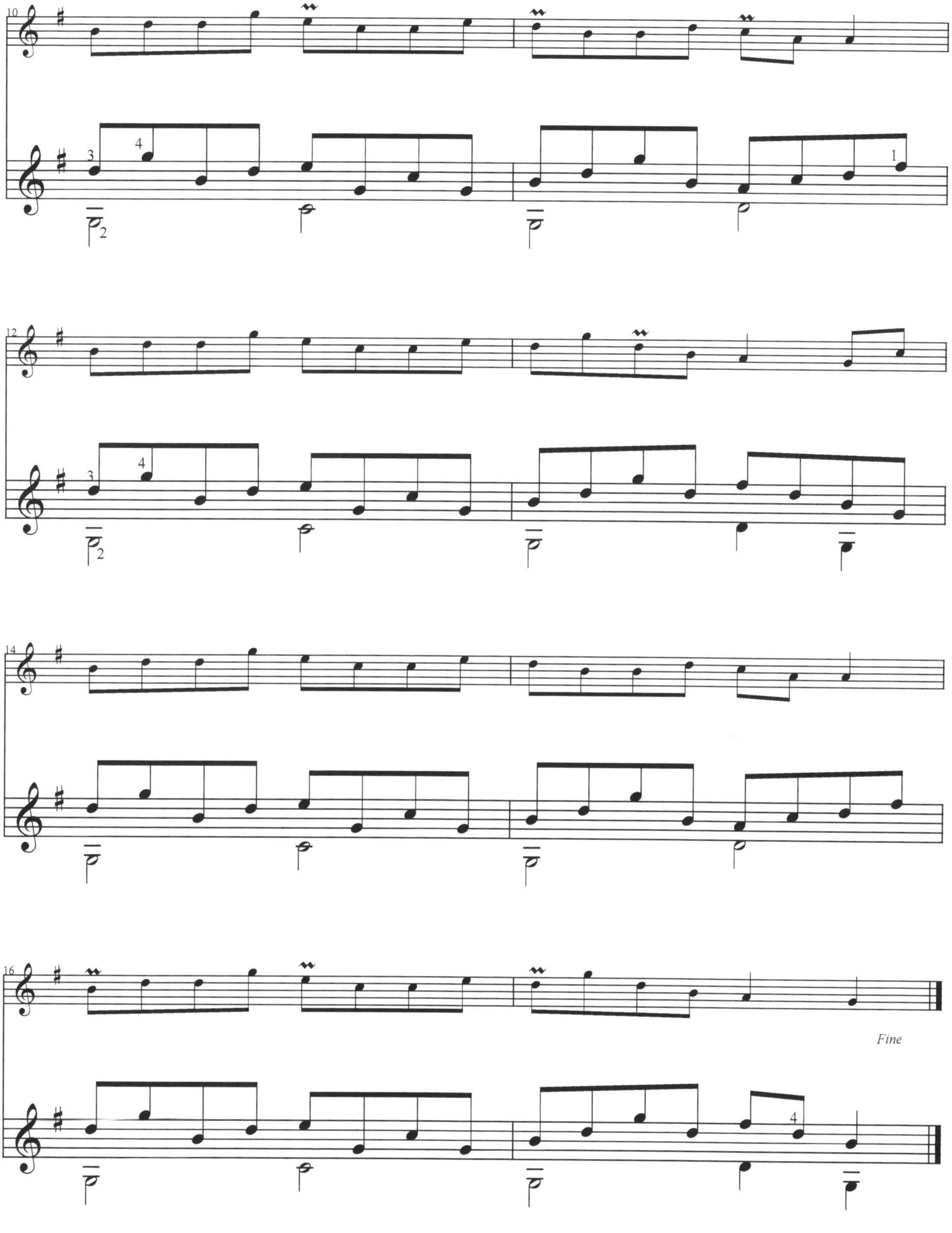
Fine

Stroketown Lasses

Hornpipe

arranged by Volker Luft

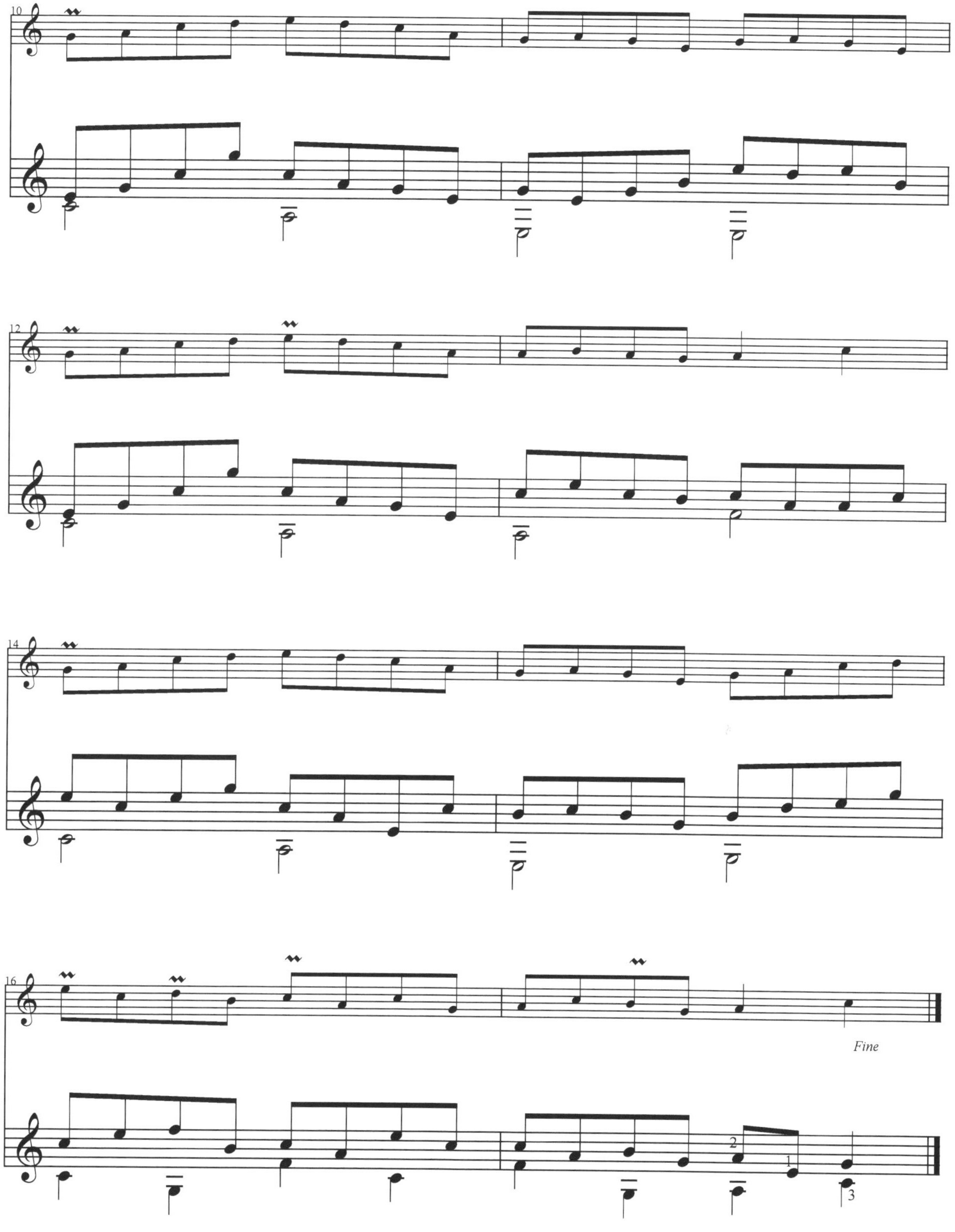
10
12
14
16
Fine

The Rakes of Castlebar

Hornpipe

arranged by Volker Luft

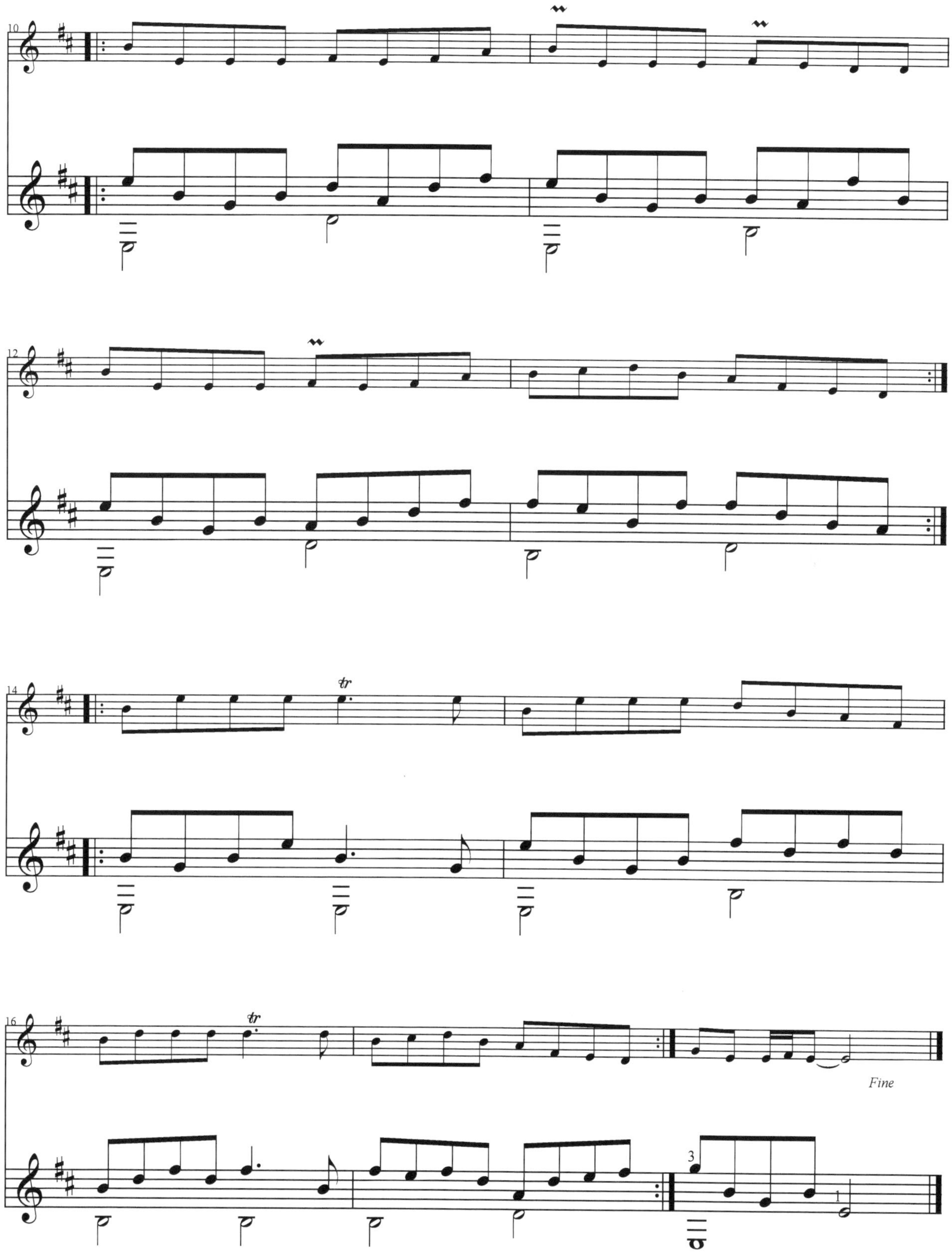
10
12
14
tr
16
tr
3
1
Fine

Made in the USA
Lexington, KY
03 September 2010